Suzy went to the playground today so happy and excited.

"We got a computer, we got a computer…" she yelled to her friends.

Clara said,"We have a computer too. I surf the web all the time."

Danny said "We have a computer too. My older sister uses it all the time."

Sam replied that he wasn't allowed to have a computer because his dad said there were monsters in computers.

Sam said "Yes, monsters in computers. My dad says there is a 'click-me' monster in computers."

Clara asked Sam, "What's a 'Click-me' monster?"

Sam Said " a 'click-me' monster is where your computer tricks you into 'clicking' something on your screen and then something bad happens to your computer"

Clara said, "I've seen that. Someone I didn't know sent me a video of a cute little dancing bear. I wasn't sure what to do with it, but my mom told me to delete it. My mom knows a lot about computers too."

Clara continued "My mom also warned me not to talk to strangers on the Internet. She said that I shouldn't tell anybody my birthday, or my address, or stuff like my phone number."

Danny said "There must be a monster in my sister's computer because she always cries and is sad whenever she uses it."

"Sounds like you have a monster in your computer. We should tell Mrs. Wright the school principal.

Danny was very quiet. He said "Mrs. Wright, I think there is a monster in my computer that's hurting my older sister." Mrs. Wright was very concerned. She leaned closer to Danny and said "Danny, tell me about your sister and why you think there's a monster in your computer." Danny replied "Whenever my sister is on the computer she is very sad and cries a lot. It's like the computer is trying to hurt her."

Mrs. Wright was very concerned about what Danny had told her. She said "Danny, it sounds like your sister is being 'cyber-bullied'. Cyber Bullying is where people use the computer to be very mean to others. Young people, just like your sister, have been really hurt by cyber bullies."

Mrs. Wright then turned to the whole group and said "you all did the right thing coming telling me about these monsters in your computers. Danny, Cyber Bullying is against the law and we need to help your sister right away before it's too late."

Mrs. Wright called the police department and asked that they investigate the cyber bullying happening to Danny's sister.

"It turned out that someone from the high school where Danny's sister went to school was 'cyber bullying' 3 different girls with her computer. Cyber Bullying is against the law and she was in big trouble."

That evening, Suzy was home for dinner.
When she saw her mother she said

"Mommy, there's monsters in our computers." Her mom asked, "What do you mean?" Suzy replied, "We met with our school principal today and we talked about it." Suzy continued,"There's the 'click-me' monster that tricks you into doing bad things to your computer. And you should never tell too much information about yourself to a stranger, especially on the Internet." "That's right" her mom replied "You need to be very careful when you're on the computer." Then Suzy said "And we helped Danny's older sister stop from being cyber-bullied by a kid from her school."

Suzy's mom put her arms around Suzy and said

"You did the right thing and I'm very proud of you. You must always let me know anytime there's a monster in our computer. I don't ever want you to get hurt by them." Then she smiled and said "OK, let's eat dinner before it gets cold."

This book is dedicated to:

Amanda Todd (15)   Megan Meier (13)

Ryan Halligan (13)   Phoebe Prince (15)

Amanda Cummings (15)   Alexis Pilkington (17)

Jamey Rodemeyer (14)   Rebecca Ann Sedgwick (12)

Chanelle Rae (14)   Erin Gallagher (13)

Hope Witsell (13)   Audrie Pott (15)

Ciara Pugsley (15)   Rehtaeh Parsons (17)

Hannah Smith (14)

Resources:

- The US Department of Homeland Security has a wonderful awareness & training program at http://www.dhs.gov/stopthinkconnect
- The Family Online Safety Institute – http://www.fosi.org/
- www.StopCyberBullying.org
- Wikipedia has some great information on Cyber Bullying: http://en.wikipedia.org/wiki/Cyber_bullying#United_States_3

Some good information on Identity Theft:

- http://www.idtheftcenter.org/index.html
- Many states have regional cybercrime organizations. An example in California is the Northern California Computer Crimes Task Force (www.NC3TF.org). Check with your local law enforcement agency to see if they handle computer crimes or if there are regional cybercrime resources in your area.
- The FBI's National Cyber Investigative Joint Task Force http://www.fbi.gov/about-us/investigate/cyber/ncijtf
- IC3.GOV

And if you want to really have your heart broken, watch the video from Amanda Todd:

- http://www.youtube.com/watch?v=vOHXGNx-E7E

About the Author:

N. K. McCarthy is a Computer Security professional and the author of "The Computer Incident Response Planning Handbook" which was published by McGraw-Hill and is available for sale at Amazon.com. He resides in Northern California with his family.

About the Illustrator:

Arthur King is currently based in Northern California, teaches drawing, painting, cartooning, illustration and animation at Diablo Valley College. His work has been shown at the Oakland Museum of California, and he maintains a comic blog about the adventures of being a dad. Oh-dad.blogspot.com. Follow him on Twitter: @arthursking

Introduction:

Dr. Abby Anderson is a clinical psychologist with a specialization in child therapy and parenting. Graduated with and M.A in psychology in 1999 and a Doctor of psychology degree in 2004. Doctor Anderson currently has a private practice in the Bay Area.